Contents

Steps to walking with Jesus

Step 1. Use this booklet to help you come to a living relationship with Jesus, and to have Him come alive within you.

Step 2. Using either "A Shower of Blessings" or "Dear Lord, I'm Desperate", (or both) for daily prayer, learn to grow in your relationship with Jesus, and to become open to the many blessings He desires to bring into your life.

Step 3. "But I get nothing out of Mass" will help you to have the Mass come alive, while "God Has A Plan For You" will help you become open to God's special plan for your life.

These booklets are advertised on page 2

It's For You Too!

In Autumn 1972 in a special spiritual experience, Jesus came very powerfully into my life. Since then He has truly been my very best Friend. Despite all my personal failures, and I have many regrets, there has been one great constant in my life - a wonderful ongoing living relationship with Jesus that has got better and better as I learned to become more and more open to it.

I can only try to find words to express how wonderful it is, to literally be in love with Jesus, and to have His love fill one's inner being.

I would not swap even one hour of this wonderful relationship for all the gold in China. Nor can I see how anything else in all the world could possibly replace it. As St. Therese of Lisieux said, " I have no wishes left at all except to love Our Lord to distraction" (Autobiography).

St. Faustina repeatedly speaks of her experience of this love-relationship with Jesus. "God drew me to Himself so strongly and powerfully that sometimes I was not aware of being on earth." (Diary 142)

"I was suddenly immersed in Him. ... Jesus filled me with such great peace that, later on, even when I tried to become uneasy, I could not do so." (Diary 143)

Yet she also explains how this can be very gentle and non-threatening:- "Jesus gives Himself to the soul in a gentle and sweet manner, and in His depths there is peace." (Diary 622)

One wonderful thing about being in love with Jesus is that both He and the Holy Spirit enter into one's inner heartroom. This is something that nobody else can do - not one's spouse, nor one's parents, nor one's best human friend, nor anyone else. Each of us have a special inner centre, the heartroom, which nobody can enter except Jesus. Unless He enters it, it remains empty.

That is why falling in love with Jesus goes way beyond any human love. Human love cannot even begin to compare with it. The presence of Jesus just fills one's inner being. It gives one a happiness that is beyond compare. It means that one is never alone, and that one eventually reaches the stage where one delights in the time that one can spend alone with Jesus.

The good news is that Jesus desires this for you too. So ask the Holy Spirit to help you to realise how wonderful it would be for you to experience this.

Pause to Pray

O Holy Spirit, please help me to realise how wonderful and how exciting it would be for me to have Jesus come alive within me.

Open my eyes as I read this booklet, so that I may become aware of how I too could become open to the most amazing experience open to humankind.

Steps in Meditation

1) Become conscious of any emptiness or lack of fulfilment or inner pain in your life at this moment.

2) Become conscious of how much you need this living relationship with Jesus.

3) Speak to Jesus and ask Him to fill your inner being.

From Despair To Joy

While I had a happy childhood, things went badly for me in boarding school. This brought a lot of sadness into my life, causing me to lose my sense of self-esteem, to turn in on myself, to develop a deep inferiority complex, and to lose my ability to concentrate.

At the end of secondary school, I felt a desire to go for the priesthood. I found Maynooth a fabulous place, and was truly amazed by the nobility of my fellow students.

In the new environment, my capacity to concentrate came back after a year or so, and my grades improved dramatically. Yet I was still struggling within myself. I was indeed to struggle for many many years with feelings of inferiority, with the lack of self-esteem, with the sense of isolation, and also with hurt and anger.

As the late Bishop Fulton Sheen so often said, "There can be no Easter Sunday without Good Friday." When our suffering becomes so great that we feel deserted even by God, that can be the very moment we become open to the power of the resurrection. Those who are blessed with special spiritual experiences, even the great saints, usually have come through a time of great desolation.

By 1972 I felt I could go no further. All the loneliness and inner emptiness came bursting to the surface. It was the same as if there was a bottomless hole in my chest, and this bottomless hole was like a vacuum sucking me in. The inner desolation was so great that I desired not to be, and so I had to fight suicidal desires.

Perhaps I was also going through what is called the 'dark night of the soul'. The increased desolation had led to real questions about my faith, and to serious doubts about

Jesus and His promises. Jesus had said, "I am the bread of life" (John 6:35), yet here I was, despite my desire to serve Him, suffering unspeakable desolation. Jesus had said, "He or she who drinks of the water that I shall give, will never thirst again" (John 4:14), yet here I was attending Mass daily even during the holidays, and receiving Him in Holy Communion, yet totally unsatisfied. Jesus had said, " I have come that you may have life, life in all its fullness", (John 10:10 GNB), yet here I was suffering real despair.

There was a clear contradiction between the claims and the promises made by Jesus and my life experience. **I found myself saying to Him, "Jesus, if you are real, then why am I experiencing this terrible desolation?"**

Meanwhile it had become obvious that, given my inner desolation, the suicidal desires, and the questions about the faith, that I could no longer continue for the priesthood, and so I had told our vocations director, and my mother and some members of my family that I was leaving.

Just then I happened to be given David Wilkerson's book, "The Cross and the Switchblade". In it, David describes how he felt led by the Holy Spirit to work amongst the street gangs in New York. He started speaking to the street gangs about the power of the Holy Spirit to transform lives. Several gang members, into all sorts of crime and hooked on drugs, had profound conversion experiences, and were delivered from their addictions by the power of the Holy spirit.

Reading "The Cross and the Switchblade" was like reading the Acts of the Apostles, except now it was happening in the modern era. As I read this book, I too received the faith to believe that my life could also be transformed by the power of the Holy Spirit. On that basis, I decided to stay in Maynooth for that year.

Shortly afterwards I was walking up the corridor in Maynooth and met a group of classmates coming down. They told me they had a minibus booked to go to a big prayer meeting in Eustace Street in Dublin, and that there was one place left, if I cared to join them. I certainly did!

There was a guest speaker there that night, a Presbyterian Minister from Belfast. He too spoke very strongly of the power of the Holy Spirit to transform lives. After the meeting I rushed up to be prayed with by him, and was disappointed when nothing appeared to happen.

The minibus was waiting, so I made a very quick exit. But even as I ran for the door with my mind very much on getting to the minibus, I noticed a little sensation of heat beginning to develop where previously I had experienced the inner emptiness, the bottomless hole. The sensation of heat gradually developed until it became a real ball of heat billowing and swirling until it filled that entire inner cavity. While David Wilkerson's book was about the power of the Holy Spirit, and the Presbyterian Minister had spoken of the Holy Spirit, I had a deep sense of being touched by Jesus. The sensation of heat lasted in some form for several days, possibly close to three weeks.

After it left, there was a sense of inner peace, and then there came a deep sense of the indwelling Jesus.

Some are completely transformed when the Holy Spirit comes upon them, and are delivered from compulsions and all sorts of things. In my case, Jesus came powerfully into my life, but every other problem I had developed, I had to learn to deal with later. I have many regrets and am deeply conscious of my own failures. There were some very difficult times even after Jesus came into my life. I also had to persevere when I appeared to be making no progress and when I found many spiritual events boring. Yet thankfully for the past 31 years, there never was a day when I didn't know the presence of Jesus, and as I worked through my difficulties, I gradually came into a most profound experience of the indwelling Jesus.

Over the years, I have seen some who had spiritual experiences fall by the wayside, while many others who never had a big experience, have come to a most profound relationship with Jesus. **Coming to a deep relationship with Jesus is not dependent on having a big experience.** It depends rather on one's willingness to keep persevering, to keep one's eyes on Jesus and to settle for nothing less - no opting for compromises.

Jesus desires to enter your life too. That is what He meant when He said, "He or she who drinks of the water that I shall give will never thirst again" (John 4:14).

There are however two questions that you need to answer:-

1) Do you really desire to come to know Jesus as your best Friend, to fall in love with Him?
2) Are you prepared to do what it takes to come to know Jesus in this way?

Pause to Pray

Lord Jesus, You promised that he or she who drinks of the water that you give will never thirst again. Lord I do desire to drink this water. I do desire to come to know you as my best Friend, and for You to become the Bread of Life for me.

Lord I am sorry for all my sins. I desire to be cleansed of all wrong inclinations, and to become open to your special plan for my life.

Nicky's Story

Nicky had always had a deep belief in God.
He was concerned about the moral decay in his country and joined a group dedicated to bringing about reform.
He was a man of prayer, praying several times a day.
He was looked up to as a leader in his faith community.
To the very best of our knowledge he had no hidden vices.

It has often struck me that if I had been speaking at his funeral, I would have pointed out all his wonderful qualities, his prayer life, his belief in God, his commitment to bringing reform, his leadership in the faith community and then I would have suggested that he had gone straight to heaven. But that was not how Jesus saw it.

Nicky's real name was Nicodemus and he went to see Jesus one night. Instead of telling Nicodemus that he was wonderful, and praising him for all his prayers and all his efforts to bring spiritual renewal, Jesus told him that he needed to make a complete fresh start, to be born again.

But what was wrong with Nicodemus faith? Why did Jesus tell him that he needed a total fresh start, a fresh start that was so basic that Jesus said that Nicodemus needed to be born again?

This is a very important question for Catholics to ask, for sometimes the way we live our faith can be very similar to that of Nicodemus. We get the first clue when Jesus says, "What is born of the flesh is flesh; what is born of the spirit is spirit" (John 3:6).

"What is born of the flesh is flesh". This is Jesus' way of telling Nicodemus that he was operating out of his own energy. His religion was **the D.I.Y. version**; do it yourself.

"What is born of the Spirit is spirit". Instead of working out of his own energy, Nicodemus needed to become open to the power of the Holy Spirit to transform his life. He needed a change that would begin on the inside; needed to have his heart transformed by the power of the Holy Spirit. Jesus was later to call this being "baptised with the Holy Spirit" (Acts 1:5). He told Nicodemus that he needed to be born again of water and the Holy Spirit.

Jesus called the Pharisees hypocrites. Today the word hypocrite has taken on a lot of derogatory baggage. It didn't have this baggage in the time of Jesus. Indeed, according to some Scripture scholars, Jesus was the first person to use the word in this sense. Back then the word hypocrite meant the same as our word 'actor', a person who gets up on the stage to act. In calling the Pharisees "hypocrites", Jesus was telling them that they were putting on a performance. Sometimes it may have been a very good performance, but it was still a performance. Their inner selves were not being transformed. It was still D.I.Y. religion, rather than becoming open to the power from on high that alone can transform our inner selves.

The passages about the Pharisees are not in the Bible to let us know how terrible the Pharisees were. They are in the Bible to warn us that **there is a wrong type of religion**, and it is very easy to slip into it. That is why Jesus warned His disciples, "Beware of the yeast of the Pharisees which is putting on a performance" (hypocrisy) (Mt. 16:16).

We Catholics, and indeed all Christians, need to look urgently at the passages about the Pharisees in the gospels, and also at the passages challenging us to rebirth and transformation. We too need to "beware of the yeast of the Pharisees which is putting on a performance".

Believing in God isn't enough. Praying isn't enough. Going to Mass isn't enough. Keeping the regulations isn't enough.

We need to become open to the full rebirth by the power of the Spirit, what Jesus was speaking about when He said, "Not many days from now you will be baptised with the Holy Spirit" (Acts 1:5). We need to learn to pray with the heart, and to allow the Holy Spirit to cleanse and transform us from within. Having received Jesus in Holy Communion, we need to allow Him to truly come to life within us, and to allow Him to so touch us in our inner selves, that we become worthy temples of His presence.

But do not be frightened. Follow the suggestions in this booklet, and you will take a mighty step towards becoming open to the full complete Baptism in the Spirit.

Pause to Pray

Lord Jesus, I thank you that I don't have to win my own salvation, that my task is to accept what You have won for me and to take the practical steps to cooperate with what You desire to do in my life.

Lord Jesus, I desire the full works; the full Baptism in the Spirit. Instead of relying on my own power, I desire to become open to Your power to transform my life. Help me to take the steps necessary to become open to it. And help me to fall in love with You.

Steps in Meditation

Accept that you cannot transform your inner self, and mentally picture yourself surrendering yourself into the hands of Jesus who desires to transform you from within.

Then mentally picture Jesus giving you all the strength you need to live a truly Christian life.

What is Baptism in the Spirit?

Before the word Baptism came to be used in the religious sense, it was a secular word with a number of meanings. It is a great help to understanding its religious meaning if we understand what it meant before it became a religious word. While the literal meaning of the word 'Baptism' was to be dipped into something, in practice there were two situations it was applied to in particular:- to be flooded with, and to be dyed through and through.

In May 2003, I led a Triduum in Blackpool in Cork City, and it was very easy to explain these two meanings of the word 'baptism' there. The river in Blackpool runs under the street. A couple of months before the Triduum the river got blocked and Blackpool was flooded. To use the word baptism in one of its original meanings, that is to be flooded, Blackpool was truly baptised, when the river got blocked under the street and erupted!

The second meaning of baptism comes from the dye trade. A garment was baptised when the dye went right through it. As it happens, Blackpool for many years had a textile industry, and the surplus dye flowed into a pool of water causing it to always look black. Hence the name Blackpool.

So the two secular meanings of the word 'baptism' were to be flooded with and to be dyed through and through. Realising this will help us greatly when we seek to understand the meaning of Baptism in the Spirit and also the graces available to us through our sacramental Baptism. And also what is required if we are to be truly born again by the power of the Holy Spirit.

We need to be flooded with the presence of Jesus, and dyed through and through with the healing, cleansing and delivering power of the Holy Spirit.

To Be Flooded With

What needs to be flooded with what?
Our inner heartroom need to be flooded with the indwelling Jesus, and with a deep sense of being loved by God.

Our heartroom is the most important element of our being. I experienced what life was like when my heartroom was empty. Then I had the experience of it being filled, the sensation of the ball of heat as Jesus touched my life. Then for the past 31 years I have been blessed with a deep sense of Jesus residing in my heartroom.

You too need to have Jesus come alive in your heartroom. How this happens will vary from person to person, just like with falling in love. With falling in love, it can be instantaneous and deeply emotional, or it can develop very slowly and steadily.

So too with coming to a living relationship with Jesus. An occasional person may be blessed with a deep experience of His presence, but for the majority, it is something that one grows into gradually, as one learns to welcome Him to live in one's heartroom. There are practical steps which one can take to help one to become open to what Jesus desires to do within us; to become open indeed to the living presence of Jesus in our heartroom.

I have described how Jesus came powerfully into my life, the experience of heat where previously I had experienced the inner emptiness, then the deep ongoing experience of the indwelling Jesus. That is how my heartroom came to be flooded with the presence of Jesus, and with a deep sense of being loved by God.

I cannot say how you will be led into this experience of the

Risen Jesus, because each person is unique, but what I can declare with 100% certainty is that it is Jesus' desire to lead you into it, and that there are practical steps which you can take to enable you to become open to Jesus.

I know that this relationship is for everyone who truly desires it from the words of Jesus Himself. In the words of Jesus, it is for "anyone (who) thirsts" and for "whoever drinks".

"I am the bread of life" (John 6:35).
"**He or she** who eats my flesh and drinks my blood lives in me and I live in him or her" (John 6:56).
"**Whoever** drinks of the water that I shall give will never thirst again. The water that I shall give him will become in him a spring of water welling up to eternal life" (John 4:14).
"**If anyone thirst**, let him come to me and drink .... out of his heart shall flow streams of living water" (John 7:38).

Early saints, like St. Hilary of Poitiers, spoke of the streams of living water flowing from one's heart once one comes to a living relationship with Jesus. Around 365, St. Hilary wrote, "When someone has drunk from the water of the Lord, then streams will flow from the heart of that person. So make sure that you drink the water of the Lord, so that the rivers will flow" (Tract on the Psalms).

Some debate as to whether it is from one's own heart or the heart of Jesus that these rivers flow. In reality once Jesus comes to live within us, then our heart comes into a special union with His heart, so it is from the union of the two hearts, ours with Jesus, that the waters flow.

St. Hilary says, "The Holy Spirit is called a river. When we receive the Holy Spirit we are made drunk. Because out of us, as a source, various streams of grace flow, the prophet prays that the Lord will inebriate us."
Again he says, "We who have been reborn through the

sacrament of Baptism experience intense joy when we feel within us the first stirrings of the Holy Spirit." (Both quotations are from St. Hilary's 'Tract on the Psalms').

Pause to Pray

Lord Jesus I desire for you to flood my heartroom with Your living presence. Fill me, O Lord, with Your love.

Lord Jesus, I do love You, and I desire to love you with all my mind, with all my heart, with all my soul and with all my strength.

Lord Jesus, I desire this not just for myself but for others also, and I pray for the grace to be able to help others to come to know you as their best Friend.

Steps in Meditation

1) Place your hands on your chest. Become conscious that Jesus is already within you. Then ask Him to truly come alive within you. Mentally picture this happening.

2) Then mentally picture a spring of water welling up within your heart; springing up and flowing out.

3) Become conscious of Jesus within you and of your heart being united with His Heart. Become conscious of rays of blessing flowing from His heart. Then, holding your needs before Him, repeat 3 times,
May Your Sacred Heart, Lord Jesus, be praised, glorified and honoured throughout the whole world now and for ever more.

4) Remaining conscious of Jesus within you, and of your heart being united with His heart, hold before Him those for whom you desire to pray, then repeat the prayer to the Sacred Heart the three times.

To Be Dyed Through

Just as in the dye trade, the dye goes right through the garment, so too in our case, our entire being needs to be penetrated through and through by the healing, cleansing and delivering power of the Holy Spirit.

This may occasionally happen by the direct gift of the Holy Spirit. When that happens, it is often like a current passing through one's body, and afterwards one knows that one has been healed, cleansed and delivered in, at least, a specific area. I experienced that in the area of my sexuality, which for years was a real struggle for me.

While spending a couple of days in prayer by the seaside, I happened to pick up and open a book. The words, "Celibacy is a gift" really lit up. At the same moment, it was as if a current passed right through my body cleansing me and setting me free from sexual compulsions.

In every other area of my life I had to learn how to become open to the healing, cleansing and delivering power of the Holy Spirit, identifying the areas in which I most needed it, and then learning how to become open to His power to set me free. (My little prayer booklet, "A Shower of Blessings" emerged from that process.)

The image the early Church Fathers used for this process was of putting a piece of iron into a fire, something they were very familiar with. As the heat penetrated the iron to its core, it became bright all through. This is the way the Holy Spirit works in the inner person.

Hand in hand with seeking to become open to the healing, cleansing and delivering power of the Holy Spirit, one should also invite Jesus to become Lord of each area of one's life. Take sexuality. Only when we have been healed of past hurts and of the consequences of our own wrong attitudes and choices, cleansed of the impact that these have had on our hormones, and delivered of our compulsions, can Jesus truly be Lord of our sexuality.

The same applies to our thoughts, our desires, our ambitions, our memories, our attitudes, our appetites, our emotions, our reflexes, our fears, etc.

Pause to Pray

O Holy Spirit I desire to become open to Your healing, cleansing and delivering power in every area of my being. (Putting your hands to your chest). **I hold before You my heart, desiring that You heal it, cleanse it, and deliver it from all compulsions, so that it may become a fitting temple for Jesus, and a true centre of love.**

Make the sign of the cross on your chest, just as it was made in Baptism, as a sign of your desire for Jesus to truly become Lord of your heart. Then let your hands relax.

I hold before You my conscience. Cleanse it, deliver it, heal it, and bring it under Your inspiration. I hold before You my will. Heal it, deliver it, cleanse it, and strengthen it to act according to Your guidance.

I hold before You my memories right back to the moment of my conception, my good memories, my painful memories, my buried memories, and the memories of my own sins, desiring that my memories may be completely penetrated by Your healing, cleansing and delivering power.

I hold before You my hopes, my plans and my ambitions desiring that they too may be penetrated,

that my hopes be transformed by Your hopes, my plans by Your plans, my ambitions by Your ambitions.

I hold before You my fears and worries, repenting of the times that I have given way to them, desiring to be delivered from all compulsions to worry or be afraid, and praying for the grace to be able to look into the eyes of Jesus, and to declare, "Jesus, I trust in You".

I hold before You my appetites and my desires, desiring that they too may be transformed by Your healing, cleansing and delivering power, and that I may be delivered from all compulsions in the area of my appetites and my desires.

I hold before You my sexuality, praying that it too may be transformed by your healing, cleansing and delivering power, that I may be set free both from hurts and from the consequences of my own sins, and that I may be delivered from sexual compulsions.

I hold before You my emotions, my attitudes and my reflexes, that they too may be penetrated by Your healing, cleansing and delivering power. May I be healed, cleansed and delivered of inner anger. May I be set free of judgementalism. May I receive the grace to be able to take the unexpected in my stride.

Place your hands on your head, asking the Holy Spirit to penetrate it with His healing cleansing and delivering power. Then make the sign of the cross on your forehead, just as it was made in Baptism and Confirmation, as a sign of your desire for Jesus to truly be Lord of very area of your mind. Then make the sign of the cross over your mouth inviting Jesus to be Lord of your tongue, and over your ears and eyes, praying that they be opened to His word.

Am I Born Again?

"I was baptised as a baby. Does this mean that I have been truly born again?"

In the early church, when it was mostly adults that were baptised, they expected to receive the baptism in the Spirit on the occasion of their Baptism. They spent a full two years preparing for Baptism, during which time they were led to expect something very special to happen.

Back then, the Baptism of Jesus was seen as the model for all Baptism. Just as Jesus had a special experience of the love of His Father, and the outpouring of the Holy Spirit on the occasion of His Baptism, they expected the same.

In fact they expected more, for **in the first place they expected to be brought into a deep union with Jesus**. This is what made all other blessings possible. It was through being united with Jesus at the moments of His death and resurrection in Baptism, that it was possible for one to become open to the love of the Father and the outpouring of the Holy Spirit.

Being immersed in the water symbolised the different elements of Baptism. Back then, there was a special room with a pool of water beside each church. One went down three steps into the water as a symbol of one's being united with the death of Jesus. Then, at the other side, one rose up three steps as a symbol of being united with the resurrection of Jesus.

One expected something very special to happen in the process:- not merely that one would come to a living relationship with Jesus and become open to the outpouring of the Holy Spirit, but also that one would be delivered from compulsions to sin. Writing about the effects of Baptism, St. Paul says, "Jesus took with Him our old selves to the cross so that we might be delivered from our compulsions to sin" (Romans 6:6).

They expected to be delivered from their compulsions at the moment of Baptism or at least, that thereafter Jesus would give them all the strength they needed to live the truly Christian life. "Reckon yourselves dead to sin but alive to God in Christ Jesus." (Romans 6:11).

Being immersed into the water was a symbol of their being flooded with the presence of Jesus and with the love of the Father, and also of their being dyed through and through with the healing, cleansing and delivering power of the Holy Spirit.

With St. Augustine, the emphasis changed to the need to be freed from Original Sin. But in the early church that was seen as a side effect. When one came up the three steps, one put on a white garment as a symbol of being united with the risen Jesus, and of the new life that one was now both called to live and empowered to live.

One then went for the very first time into Mass. Before one was baptised, one had to leave Mass after the readings and homily. What takes place during the Eucharistic Prayer was seen as being such a great mystery that only those who had been properly prepared and then enlightened through the graces of Baptism could begin to understand it. Baptism was thus also seen as, and sometimes called, the **sacrament of enlightenment**. It was the sacrament which opened the eyes of the mind and heart. After Baptism the eyes of the mind and heart were enlightened to see spiritual things in a new way. Thus they could begin to perceive how the Mass, like Baptism, made present the death and resurrection of Jesus, and how the bread and wine truly became the body and blood of the risen Jesus.

Now too for the very first time, they could receive the risen Jesus in Holy Communion. Having already been immersed into His death and resurrection during Baptism, and enlightened to recognise what happens during the great mystery of the Mass, they were ready to recognise the bread and wine as the body and blood of Jesus.

It is interesting that in the modern era, many people have testified that after receiving the Baptism in the Spirit, the Scriptures, etc. began to light up for them in a new way. The eye of the mind had been enlightened so that both the Bible and spiritual events come alive in a new way.

We were baptised as infants and confirmed, often without much preparation, as children. However the good news is that we don't have to miss out. We too can come into everything that they experienced in the early church.

Even the apostles did not receive the outpouring of the Holy Spirit when they were baptised. In John's Gospel, immediately after Jesus told Nicodemus that he needed to be born again of water and the Holy Spirit, it is recorded, "After this Jesus and his disciples went into the land of Judea; there He remained with them and baptised." (John 3:22 RSV). The clear implication of this is that the apostles were baptised by Jesus. This appears to have been a special time that He spent with the disciples and that Baptism was the central feature.

Thus the Apostles were baptised by Jesus, but they did not receive the full Baptism in the Spirit until Pentecost. They were baptised first and received the outpouring of the Spirit later. For some people in the Acts of the Apostles, it happened the other way around. They actually received the outpouring of the Holy Spirit before they were baptised. So the two do not have to happen at the one time.

Speaking around the year 348 of what the Apostles experienced at Pentecost, St. Cyril of Jerusalem says, "The disciples were within and the whole house was filled. Therefore they were **baptised without anything wanting**, according to the promise." (Cathecetical Lectures)

So even though they had already been baptised in the Jordan, they were now baptised again by the power of the Holy Spirit, this time "without anything wanting". 'The promise' refers to what Jesus had promised, "Not many days from now you will be baptised with the Holy Spirit."

The phrase "baptised without anything wanting" implies that it is possible to be baptised but yet that something could still be wanting. Just indeed as the Apostles had been baptised, but had not received the outpouring of the Holy Spirit, so too it is possible for us to have been baptised and even confirmed, but yet not come into the fullness of the new life that Jesus desires for us even here and now.

There are indeed millions of people who have been baptised and confirmed, but whose lives do not manifest the type of relationship with either the Father, Son or Holy Spirit that one might reasonable expect of a person who had been truly "born again of water and the Holy Spirit". Likewise there are many people who can testify, like myself, that at one stage they were committed believers, but later on came into a profound new experience of what it is to be "born again of water and the Holy Spirit".

The good news is that Jesus desires,
A) To draw you into a living relationship with Himself, so

that you will know Him as your best Friend, and so that you will actually experience Him as the Bread of Life, experience what He promised when He said, "Whoever drinks of the water that I shall give will never thirst again. The water that I shall give him will become in him a spring of water welling up to eternal life" (John 4:14).

B) For you to become open to the healing, cleansing and delivering power of the Holy Spirit,

C) That you will know how much the Father loves you and that your sins are forgiven.

To become open to this, doing some programme is often necessary. Many, even non Charismatics, find the "Life in the Spirit Seminars" very helpful. For others it has happened during the Alpha programme. For others it has been at a weekend retreat or Marriage Encounter. For others it has been in Medjugorje or some other place of pilgrimage. For others it has been while reading a book or even a booklet like this.

I can only encourage you to decide that this is something that you want and that you will seek it until you find it.

Pause to Pray

Lord Jesus, I desire to become open to the full Baptism in the Spirit. Please make it possible for me. Help me to take the steps necessary to become open to it.

Steps in Meditation

Picture yourself being in the room with the Apostles and Our Lady at Pentecost. Ask Our Lady, who prayed for the apostles to receive the full Baptism in the Spirit, to pray that you too may also receive it. Become conscious of your desire to become open to everything. Tell Jesus that you want everything, the full works.

To Meet The Risen Jesus

It is wonderful when the breakthrough to a vibrant living relationship with Jesus comes instantly, but how do you become open to it, when it doesn't? **The good news is that coming to a living relationship with Jesus does not depend upon one having a big initial experience**.

It is right to take part in a programme where there is an expectation that your life will be touched in a special way. I very strongly recommend that you do so. Coming to a living relationship with Jesus is the most wonderful thing that can happen in your life.

Think of what you would be prepared to do to come into a million euro! You would be prepared to travel a great distance, to take part in any sort of prolonged programme, to work long hours, etc.

I can assure you that those who have really come to a living relationship with Jesus would not be prepared to swap that for a thousand million euro - or indeed for all the money that was ever made.

It is truly the most wonderful, the most exhilarating, the most liberating, the most fulfilling experience open to humankind.

Far better than drugs and there are no bad side effects!

So, do go to special places and events if it is humanly possible at all. Some people will have special experiences, especially when being prayed with for the Baptism in the Spirit. Others will not have special experiences, but some will know afterwards that there is a difference - they will find it easier to pray or find the New Testament lighting up in a new way, or notice a new level of joy in their lives.

For others, nothing will appear to have changed. If that is your experience, remember **Jesus loves you as much as He loves the person who has a deep experience**. It is just that your needs and personality are different.

He desires for you to come to a living relationship with Him. He desires that for you far more than you desire it for yourself. Just because you don't have a big experience at the beginning of the journey does not mean that you won't grow to the heights. St. Therese of Lisieux did not have a big experience in that sense, yet she was to grow and grow until she could say "I love Our Lord to distraction".

So proceed with total trust that Jesus IS going to lead you into this wonderful relationship with Himself.

He said, "I am the bread of life" (John 6:35), so keep trusting that He desires to become the bread of life for you. He said, "He or she who drinks of the water that I shall give will never thirst again" (John 4:13), so keep trusting that He desires to give you this life-giving water.

Equally you can be 100% sure that Jesus is with you right now. He Himself promised, "Behold, I am with you always." (Mt. 28:20).

Not merely is He with you, but He is within you. "He or she who eats my flesh and drinks My blood lives in Me and I live in him or her" (John 6:56).

So whether you have a spiritual experience or don't have a spiritual experience, start operating on the basis of these three totally definite truths:-

1) **Jesus desires to enter your life** in a very special way.
2) **He IS with you,** regardless of how you feel.
3) **He is actually within you**, at this very moment, even if your sense of His presence has yet to come alive.

Pause to Pray

Lord Jesus, I accept in faith that You are within me. I long for the day when I will truly experience your presence; when I will truly know you as my best Friend.

Grant me the grace to never give up until You fill my inner heartroom. Inspire me to go to the right places, read the right books, and attend the right events.

Steps in Meditation

1) Put your hands to your chest again. Realising that Jesus is in there, desire for Him to really come alive within you.

2) Form a mental picture of an explosion of God's love occurring within you. Picture it as a real explosion of love at the centre of your being.

3) Mentally picture rays of blessing surging forth from this inner explosion of God's love to penetrate every area of your heart, of your mind, and of your entire being.

Pause and slowly repeat these steps. Decide that you will repeat them regularly.

A Possible Further Meditation

First recall the sense of awe you have during Exposition. Then close your eyes, and using the eye of your mind, mentally picture the interior of your chest. Become conscious that Jesus is in there, body, blood, soul and divinity. Allow your sense of awe to return. Then mentally picture Him coming alive within you.

Mentally picture a symbol of His Lordship (perhaps a cross) being erected over your heart, and your heart being united to His heart; then of rays coming forth from the union.

Have Jesus Come Alive

Sr. Briege McKenna received a phonecall late one night. It was from a young priest, clearly distressed.

What Sr. Briege didn't know was that the priest in question had been going through a very troubled period. Effectively he was on the way out of the priesthood, and only celebrated Mass when he was on official duty.

The reason for his distress however was different. He had just been told that he had cancer of the throat. The doctors had given him the full extent of the bad news. With treatment, he could live for two years. Not having a deep relationship with Jesus, he was devastated.

Sr. Briege often gets little images when praying with people. Now she received an image of the young priest receiving Holy Communion and of healing taking place as the Sacred Host travelled down through his throat.

This gave her the confidence to say to him:- "Tomorrow morning you will be receiving Jesus in Holy Communion. He is the one who can heal you. When the Sacred Host is going down through your throat, it will be going right by where the cancer is. Ask Jesus to heal you then".

Sr. Briege then reminded him of the woman who touched the hem of the garment of Jesus. "Hundreds of people were touching Him, but just the one woman had the faith to believe her life could be transformed. Tomorrow morning, when you are receiving Holy Communion, you will have a far greater privilege than the woman who touched the hem of His garment. You will have Jesus coming to live within you".

Sr. Briege didn't know that he hadn't planned to celebrate

Mass the following morning. However inspired by her words, he got together some of his friends and celebrated Mass, paying special attention to receiving Holy Communion, to the Sacred Host as it entered his mouth and went down through his throat, asking Jesus to deliver him from cancer. Praise God a mighty miracle took place. When he went back to the hospital, there was no trace of the cancer. Not merely that, but his priesthood was renewed, and he became an inspiration to many.

(Strangely he died in a car crash two years later, around the time he would have died had the cancer taken its course. But in those wonderful two years, he had touched the lives of thousands including many young priests.)

As it happens, what Sr. Briege was inspired to say to him, about becoming conscious of Jesus present in his mouth and in his throat, reveals a truth that we so often miss.

We have great reverence for the Sacred Host in Exposition, but little realisation that Jesus really comes to us who receive.

If the risen Jesus is present in the Sacred Host, body, blood, soul and divinity, then He comes to live in you, body, blood, soul and divinity. What a mind blowing realisation that Jesus is present within you, body, blood, soul and divinity.

Before you receive, call to mind the sense of awe you have when the Sacred Host is exposed. Then as you receive, cultivate an even greater sense of awe at Jesus being really present in the Host in your hand, then in your mouth, then going down into your inner self.

Even now call to mind the last time you received Holy Communion. Jesus has not left you. He is within you. Become aware of the wonder of it.

Isn't it truly awesome, indeed beyond words, that Jesus, our Lord, our God, our Saviour actually lives within us.

But remember it is the Risen Jesus you receive, and the Risen Jesus who comes to live within us. In His recent encyclical, Pope John Paul makes this point very clearly. He says, "The flesh of the Son of Man, given as food, is his body in its glorious state after the resurrection. With the Eucharist we digest, as it were, the "secret" of the resurrection."

It is the Risen Jesus who makes Himself present under the form of bread and wine. It is the same Jesus who was able to appear in the room where the disciples were despite the doors being locked. The Jesus who was and is able to go through stone walls, yet is very real, so real that He could invite Thomas to put his hands into the wounds in his hands and side. This is the Jesus we receive.

The various Eucharistic Miracles, bleeding Hosts etc. need to be seen in this light. Just as Jesus revealed Himself to Thomas, showing him the wounds in His side and hands, so too, to assist our faith, He can cause Hosts to bleed or turn into flesh. This however should only be seen as a symbol. For the Jesus who comes to us in Holy Communion is the Risen Jesus, the Jesus whose body and blood are now glorified into their resurrected condition - no longer the earthly flesh and blood that is subject to decay.

Resurrected, glorified, yet totally real, the Risen Jesus comes to live in us.

If only we were to begin to pay as much attention to His real presence within us when we receive, and to how He desires to truly come to life within us and to transform our lives, the difference would be immense.

Pause to Pray

Lord Jesus, give me faith like the faith of the woman who touched the hem of your garment.
Give me a sense of awe as I hold the Sacred Host, as I place it on my tongue, and then as I swallow it, that it really is You, the Risen Jesus, body, blood, soul and divinity.
Help me to realise that You really do live in me; that I am actually Your living tabernacle, Your living temple.

Steps in Meditation

1) Just as the woman touched the hem of the garment of Jesus, please place your hands on your chest again.

2) Become conscious that Jesus is within you, body, blood, soul and divinity.

3) With a consciousness that Jesus is in there, become conscious also of your own sense of feeling in the depths of your chest. Take a deep breath if necessary to get a sense of inner feeling. Now desire for Jesus to truly come alive within you. Feel this desire and remain with it for as long as is comfortable.

4) Express your desire in words. Talk to Jesus. Tell Him how much you desire for Him to come alive within you. Express your love for Him, and your desire that your heart be filled with love for Him.

5) Conclude the exercise by making the sign of the cross on your chest, just as it was made in Baptism by the priest, inviting Jesus to truly be Lord of your heart.

A Prayer With Power

By His death Jesus has won for us the right to be set free from our compulsions and enslavement to sin. St. Paul tells us that the power available to transform our lives is the same power by which Jesus was raised from the dead.

The very centre of the Christian life is learning to become united with the death of Jesus so that we may become open to this mighty power of His resurrection, and, at the same time, to the outpouring of the Holy Spirit.

In the early Church, when one was being baptised, one went down three steps into the water as a symbol of being united with the death of Jesus, and then came up three steps at the other side of the baptismal pool, as a symbol of being united with the resurrection of Jesus.

At Mass we again join with Jesus in His death and resurrection. In Holy Communion we receive the Risen Jesus, body, blood, soul and divinity.

So being united with the death and resurrection of Jesus is at the very centre of the Christian life.

We bring our imperfections to Jesus, so that a real dying to selfishness and rising to new life may take place within us. The Divine Mercy Chaplet continuously unites us to the death and resurrection of Jesus, and hence to the graces of both our Baptism and the Mass, and draws us into an ever closer relationship with the Father.

On earth, Jesus taught His disciples to pray the Our Father, and gave a powerful example of ongoing prayer to the Father. Interestingly when He gave this special prayer to St. Faustina for us, it is again totally focused on the Father.

On the Our Father beads of the rosary, one prays "Eternal Father, I offer You the body and blood, soul and divinity of Your dearly beloved Son, Our Lord Jesus Christ in atonement for our sins and the sins of the whole world".

On the Hail Mary beads one prays, "For the sake of His sorrowful passion", (Response) "Have mercy on us and on the whole world".

When we pray, "I offer You the body and blood, soul and divinity of ... Our Lord Jesus Christ", become conscious that in Holy Communion you have received the body and blood, soul and divinity of our Lord Jesus Christ.

Become conscious of Jesus within you. Have a desire for Him to really come to life within you. Then offer Jesus within you to the Father and yourself in union with Him.

This is also a most beautiful prayer to say on its own after Communion while deeply conscious of the presence of Jesus within you, body, blood, soul, and divinity.

When you pray, "For the sake of His sorrowful passion, have mercy on us ...", the phrase "His sorrowful passion" includes all the events surrounding the death of Jesus; so desire to unite yourself and all your sufferings including your temptations, with His suffering and death.

Jesus took with Him to the cross your old self. He has won for you the right to be set free of your compulsions. As you pray 'have mercy on us', **have a desire to be set free from every compulsion to sin**. Desire indeed to experience the full transforming power of God.

A further image is **the vision** which St. Faustina herself had on Corpus Christi in 1937. As she was praying before the Blessed Sacrament and before the image of Divine Mercy, she had a vision of rays of mercy coming from the heart of Jesus, then flowing out through the Sacred Host, then coming out to immerse herself, and then spreading out all over the world, and she received the message that it was the desire of Jesus for everyone to experience this.

So as you pray the Chaplet, mentally picture the rays of blessing coming from the heart of Jesus to immerse you, or to immerse the people you are praying for.

It is an especially powerful prayer to offer for a person's spiritual welfare. Mentally picture the rays of mercy and blessing immersing them as you pray.

So there are 3 steps or images.

1) Mentally picture the rays of blessing coming from the heart of Jesus to immerse you and your intentions.

2) When praying "Eternal Father, I offer you the body and blood, soul and divinity ..." become conscious of Jesus within you, and that you are offering Jesus within you and your life in union with His to the Father.

3) When praying "For the sake of His sorrowful passion ..." have a sense of being united with the death and resurrection of Jesus, and desire for your life to be totally transformed, or else for whoever you are praying for to be immersed by the rays of blessing coming from the heart of Jesus.

When you pray like this, mighty blessings will be released.

Footnote:- you don't have to offer the entire chaplet all at once. I regularly intersperse a decade of it here and there when using my own booklets "A Shower of Blessings" and "Dear Lord, I'm Desperate", and again when I'm out walking.